The Trail of Unexpected Gifts

Courtney J. Strong

ILLUSTRATED BY
Carissa Robertson

To Hunter and Paisley
. . . with my whole heart, pen, and imagination . . .

The Trail of Unexpected Gifts

Copyright © 2023 by Courtney Strong
Illustrated by Carissa Robertson

Published by Lucid Books in Houston, TX
www.LucidBooks.com

ISBN: 978-1-63296-988-0 (paperback)   ISBN: 978-1-63296-622-3 (hardback)   eISBN: 978-1-63296-623-0 (ebook)

Unless otherwise indicated, all Scripture quotations are taken from the New Life Version, Copyright © 1969 and 2003. Used by permission of Barbour Publishing, Inc., Uhrichsville, Ohio 44683. All rights reserved.

Scripture quotations marked (ESV) are taken from the ESV® Bible (The Holy Bible, English Standard Version®), copyright © 2001 by Crossway, a publishing ministry of Good News Publishers. Used by permission. All rights reserved.

Scripture quotations marked (NLT) are taken from the Holy Bible, New Living Translation, copyright ©1996, 2004, 2015 by Tyndale House Foundation. Used by permission of Tyndale House Publishers, Carol Stream, Illinois 60188. All rights reserved.

Special Sales: Lucid Books titles are available in special quantity discounts. Custom imprinting or excerpting can also be done to fit special needs. Contact Lucid Books at Info@LucidBooks.com

It wasn't the comforting warmth of Dad's crackling fire, or even the gooey, long-awaited taste of Mom's sugar cookies that made young Ralph's insides jump with excitement.

It was the "tinker, tinker, clank, clank" sound of his sister's spoon in her special mug as she swirled around her hot cocoa that acted as an annual dinner bell, alerting him that Christmastime had officially begun.

In the Applegate family, Christmastime began the first night the tree was up, complete with the show-stopping star and every ounce of their MOM's energy ensuring every last MEMORY was displayed.

It was almost tradition for the back of the tree to not hold as many ornaments as the front.

Mrs. Applegate could never seem to choose any special ornaments for the back of the tree. She just couldn't bear the thought that you might go the entire holiday without seeing them.

She couldn't prioritize Ralph's second grade salt dough candy cane over their "first home" ornament. So while the back of the tree looked like simple elegance, the front of the tree welcomed anyone who entered the house with a sentimental splash and a colorful collage.

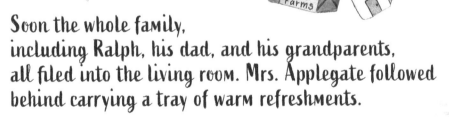

Soon the whole family, including Ralph, his dad, and his grandparents, all filed into the living room. Mrs. Applegate followed behind carrying a tray of warm refreshments.

They marched into an already cozy scene with Ralph's sister, Mallory, carefully concentrating and pausing for small tastes of her drink, trying her best to make the final marshmallow last as long as possible.

Dad's tender, yet hard-working hands slid a dusty, wooden box towards the middle of the room. Ralph and Mallory grinned like they had just run into old friends as they lifted out board books from their toddler days.

Chapter books holding those stories of miracles that would come at just the right time on Christmas Eve toppled out in jolly piles.

Oddly enough, one stowaway Thanksgiving book always made its way into the box.

This stapled-together, homemade book with hand drawings was considered a prized story. It contained Ralph and Mallory's disastrous account of when they attempted to make the holiday feast all by themselves.

Finally, the cherished family albums came out from the bottom of the box.

Ralph peacefully traced an inscription at the bottom of the empty box with his fingers. Long ago, his talented Uncle Jimmy had hand-carved the phrase "The Best is Yet to Come" inside this box which now forever held some of their favorite holiday traditions.

As Ralph traced the familiar etching, the adults acted as enthusiastic as the children, eagerly reaching for pictures that jogged individual memories, laughing and each chiming in, their voices one on top of the other with the old stories.

To their surprise, each year, someone in their family always had at least one new story to offer. Since the old pictures seemed to spark each tale, Ralph wondered if they would reach the end of new stories one day when they finished looking through all of the albums.

Mr. Applegate picked up a ruby red album. The title reading "GIFTS" appeared on the outside hardcover in black permanent marker surrounded by doodles of holly. As he flipped through the book, a piece of notebook paper yellowed with age fell onto the floor.

"Here's our next story," he announced. His eyes lit up in a way that invited attention. Everyone quieted and turned towards Ralph and Mallory's dad.

"While there are not many pictures to support this story, there is *this*," he said, as he held up a second, similar-looking sheet of paper. Grandpa let out a quiet laugh and covered his forehead with his hand in a playful wave of remembrance.

Mr. Applegate began to explain the papers, which merely looked like a list of dollar amounts and survey sketches.

"When I was a little boy, my daddy," he said looking again at smiling Grandpa, "used all of his money to chase a dream put on his **heart by God.**"

"He wanted to own a farm — land — out in the country.
But we were in the city," Grandma happily added on to the story.

"But Dad had a vision," Mr. Applegate continued.
"A vision, a dream, an idea
many people didn't understand.
And there were times he didn't even understand!

People told him if he moved from the city, he would be leaving so much he was used to. So many favorable things he was used to. At some point, he faced the truth of what others said.

He would be giving up so much. But was it too much?

The risk was high, but the dream was higher. The truth is, Grandpa saw something that some people just didn't see. Something they couldn't see. He saw more time for family and a slower rhythm. He saw a place to hold family gatherings, a place to raise animals, and more importantly, children. He saw a place to have friends and community."

"You're talking about Sunday Drive Farms, right?" Mallory asked cheerfully.

Grandpa whispered as he put his arm around Ralph. "Yes, right over there." He pointed out the window at a snow-covered path with rainbow lights illuminating the trail to their grandparents' cottage.

Ralph turned the next page just as the doorbell rang. Sauntering into the breezeway was Uncle Jimmy, the loyal and kind businessman. His shirt, tie, and clean-cut appearance was a stark contrast to his picture the family just landed upon in the memory book.

"You had a hard Christmas that year, didn't you?"

Mr. Applegate greeted his brother-in-law as he pointed to the picture and held up the album.

With his bandaged leg, his unrecognizable sleepy eyes, and a thermometer sticking up out of his mouth, Jimmy definitely stood out in the family photo book that year.

"Oh, but it was one of the best," he shared confidently.

Mallory's dad went on to reminisce about how the moment Uncle Jimmy found out the family was getting a baby girl, he was determined to build her a storybook cottage playhouse.

"Yeah, it would have been nice if I had remained in one piece and healthy...but it was worth it for the princess," Jimmy snickered as he bent over to tickle Mallory as if he didn't have a care in the world.

Mallory giggled freely. When she caught her breath, she sat dreamily with her hand over her heart. She loved hearing the "history of her castle" as she liked to call it.

"Please continue," she requested in a royal voice.

Mrs. Applegate continued with her version, "Later, even though Mallory was a newborn who just wanted to sleep, and even months later only wanted shiny objects with literal bells and whistles, Jimmy kept building a sturdy, brown wooden house for you, Mallory.

And if that wasn't enough, even the winter freeze that had him bordering on pneumonia and a broken leg after falling down on the job at the final stage of the project— didn't stop him."

Mallory's graceful hands changed into a pose of anxious fists over her heart for her uncle.

It was hard to hear the details about how Uncle Jimmy went through so much pain for her. And although she could not exactly know the fullness of the pain as a young girl, she understood enough to feel some of the weight he carried for her.

As that part of the story ended, she relaxed her hands as she longed to hold her Christmas mug again, all the while keeping her eyes on the storyteller. She moved her head down for another sip.

"Aohhhhhumph!" she exclaimed, pushing a fluffy tail away from the edge of her mug where her spoon had just been resting.

Wide-eyed, she looked into her ceramic treasure as if someone had stolen her very last lick of marshmallow. And in fact, it appeared someone was trying. Mallory saw Shipley, the Applegates' blonde kitten, sniffing and prancing around Mallory's cup with her tail sticking straight up—now sticky paws and all.

Mrs. Applegate squealed at Shipley's timely antics, and everyone else joined in, laughing out loud. Ralph and Mallory's mom tried tried to grab Shipley and clean her paws a bit, but Shipley skittered away.

Laughing again, Mrs. Applegate continued with the book of gifts, "And then there's this Christmas gift..." she said happily.

"I'm glad you are still smiling about it after all of these years," Mr. Applegate jumped in.

Ralph peered over the album to get a glimpse at this mysterious gift.

"It's..."
he began, confused,
"a hole?"

"A hole?

A donut hole?

I'd like one for Christmas!"

Mallory enthusiastically blurted out, as she reached for a pen to add "donut hole" to her Christmas list, conveniently located in the living room at her disposal.

"It really was a hole," Mr. Applegate continued.

"It was Christmas Eve, and all of your mom's friends thought surely I was going to propose that night. They were right—I did propose, but it didn't end exactly as they thought. When they heard I asked your mom to marry me, they naturally looked for a diamond on her left hand."

"And he did get a gorgeous diamond for me a few months later when he saved up the money," Mrs. Applegate said blissfully, pointing to the picture. "But first, he gave me this dirt hole."

Ralph recognized the tree beside the huge dirt hole. That's our pond, Ralph thought to himself.

It was the dirt hole that eventually filled into a pond beside their house.

"I saw much more than dirt that day," Ralph and Mallory's mom explained. "I could see future weddings beside that pond, fathers and sons fishing, people in chairs all around the water having Bible studies and retreats. And my favorite—out of all the ones that have come true—family walks around what would one day become a pond.

Of course, it was easy to see all of the good that could come from a diamond ring. It was harder to explain to my friends that he gave me a hole. But what a gift it became."

The page turned.

Ralph started thinking silently to himself about all of these stories. It seemed these types of visions his grandfather came up with had continued in the family and passed down to Ralph's father and uncle.

Every year, it was a huge deal for both Ralph and Mallory to think of Christmas presents (big or small) that would be true surprises to their family.

How did they do this? Ralph pondered his family's talent and imagination in amazement.

"So," Ralph continued.

"Grandpa, if you showed Dad and Uncle Jimmy how to dream these big dreams, then who showed you?

I mean, who started these ideas...

who was the first person to begin thinking of these gifts that no one would ever guess?"

"That's an excellent question, Ralph." Grandpa answered. "Stepping out in faith, having these big ideas...surely you can know these dreams and this way of thinking did not start with us. These were not our original plans. A long, long time ago they came from Someone more creative and more courageous and more generous than anyone in our entire family," Grandpa stated without a doubt.

"More creative than Uncle Jimmy?" Mallory said, excitedly puzzled.

"Couldn't be more courageous than Grandpa,"
Ralph stated softly with just as much assurance.

Mallory tugged on her dad's sleeve, "More generous than you, Daddy?"

Grandpa chimed in, "Actually, yes. And maybe to give you a better picture, I should say it was more than one person..."

"Oh! Oh! Oh!" Mallory interjected.
"Was it three people like Uncle Jimmy, Daddy, and you, Grandpa?"

"Well, now..." Grandpa chuckled, "I guess you could say that. Although, the kind of gift ideas They thought up...are way beyond what we ever dreamed of."

"Now, exactly how long ago are we talking about, Grandpa?" Ralph asked.

"Well," Grandpa continued. "You know how sometimes you think as far back as you can imagine, like to the beginning of the Bible when it says 'In the beginning, God created the heavens and the earth?'" He paused. The children nodded in expectation. "I'm positive it was even before that."

The family audience sat wide-eyed; the children were edging closer and closer to the their grandpa's chair.

"The Bible says that God the Father, Jesus, and the Spirit of God were all at creation — The Three I was talking about, Mallory.

They gave us the inspiration for the gifts.

Multiple places in the Bible tell us that before creation, there was a rescue plan put in place, a huge gift thought out for you."

Ralph suddenly spoke up. "It reminds me of that story, Grandpa!" The young boy shifted eagerly and sat up on his knees.

"The one we talked about the other day where Elisha was facing that huge enemy army of men, but he wasn't afraid because God allowed him to see the heavenly army that surrounded him was even bigger.

Remember, Grandpa?"

His Grandpa's eyes twinkled. He definitely remembered.

It was from 2 Kings 6, and the two of them had a great discussion over the story just a few weeks ago.

"This is just like that!

God showed you and Dad something that was . . .
that was . . .
so different from what you would normally see.
He gave you these ideas.
And He helped you do them!" Ralph exclaimed.

"It's like the 'That Makes Me Think Of' game, Grandpa!"
Mallory gladly pointed out.

"Yes and yes!" their grandpa gladly
answered both grandkids.

Grandpa taught them this fun pass around game where their answers can be silly, but it was also used to teach them an important skill.

When God shows you something in His Word, sometimes He shows it to you again in real life —just in another way.

Grandpa was elated to hear the connection this made in Ralph's heart.

"You know," Grandpa lowered his voice and leaned forward as he always did when he told his favorite part of a story.

"When I was little, one December night I overheard my parents talking in the kitchen. They had a small stack of mail, a notepad containing numbers for paying bills, and another paper where they were compiling a Christmas shopping list.

I'll never forget that night.

Of course, I was not supposed to be awake, but I remember stopping just shy of the swinging wooden doors leading into the kitchen when I heard my parents talk about the bike they wanted to get me for Christmas. And it wasn't just any bike. It was the shiny, red 10-speed bike in the window of Paddywack's Department Store.

It was the only one the store had for the season, and the shop owner wanted a lot for it, too. I heard my parents calculate how much it would cost and compared it to how much they would have at the end of the month after paying the family bills.

I knew I needed to get to bed before getting caught, but I'll never forget the phrase I heard as I tiptoed away, 'Let's go through with the plan.'"

"Did you get it, Grandpa? Did you get the bike?"
Ralph eagerly asked, his heart now racing.

"Yes, I got it. And I adored it and rode it for years.

That particular Christmas has followed me all of my life. It always reminded me of what it must have been like for the Father, Jesus, and the Spirit to imagine before the foundation of the world that Jesus would be the ransom, the price, for my sins.

Let's read directly from the best Book of all time.

This is one of my favorite passages in the Bible.

You might say it's one that magnificently describes Jesus' gift to us."

Their grandpa leaned over to grab a Bible from the top of the fireplace.

"Ephesians 1:4-9 says,

'Even before the world was made, God chose us for Himself because of His love. He planned that we should be holy and without blame as He sees us.

God already planned to have us as His own children. This was done by Jesus Christ. In His plan God wanted this done.

We thank God for His loving-favor to us. He gave this loving-favor to us through His much-loved Son.

Because of the blood of Christ, we are bought and made free from the punishment of sin. And because of His blood, our sins are forgiven.

His loving-favor to us is so rich. He was so willing to give all of this to us. He did this with wisdom and understanding.

God told us the secret of what He wanted to do.

It is this:

In loving thought He planned long ago
to send Christ into the world.'"

"With wisdom and understanding," he repeated. "This means They knew all about what this would cost. Jesus calculated the cost of waiting so long for people to understand.

The manger in Bethlehem wasn't exactly a shiny palace.

The Father, Jesus, and the Spirit knew exactly what this would cost Them— leaving the riches of heaven,

the physical hurt, and not to mention, the emotional pain of being separated."

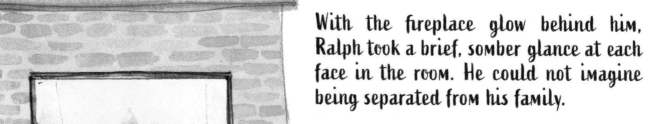

With the fireplace glow behind him, Ralph took a brief, somber glance at each face in the room. He could not imagine being separated from his family.

"But for you,"
Grandpa's bright, blue eyes looked deeply
into Ralph's face and then Mallory's.

"But for you, God said,
'Let's go through with the plan.'"

Ralph glanced happily out of the living room window. The sky was even darker now, and the rainbow lights leading to Sunday Drive Farms radiated just a little more, leading the way with even more whimsical wonder.

Mrs. Applegate started collecting dishes while Grandma and Grandpa passed out hugs. Ralph dusted off the sugar cookie crumbs from his red pajamas.

The Applegate family seemed to be slowing down for the evening. Mallory took one more glance at the family book, as if preparing to wish it goodnight. They had always been there, but this was the first year she noticed there were several extra, empty plastic sleeves in the family photo album of gifts.

Ralph glanced over at the blank pages in her hands, and he realized he never noticed them before either.

On the inside, Ralph felt like a perfectly twisted candy cane—an equal blend of peace and excitement. Ralph's eyes met Mallory's, and he knew she felt it too. He knew in his heart he and his sister would add many more pictures in the years to come.

For once, they didn't mind the thought of going to bed—they had lots they wanted to think about as they laid down.

The stories would not run out. The best surely was yet to come.

Because the best-planned, unguessable gift
had been delivered and received.

Jesus—the unexpected gift—had come!

It was time to celebrate because even though...knowing all it would cost...

They went through with the plan.

You are invited to six nights of family activities with this story.

Experience this in your own living room...just like the Applegates!

Take six nights in a row or close together during the Christmas Advent season to sit down and enjoy. Each night will include a Bible passage relating to the story for family discussion and a family experience.

NIGHT 1: Discuss the following Scriptures:
(take a peek at the activity before starting this!)

Ephesians 1:4-9

"Even before the world was made, God chose us for Himself because of His love. He planned that we should be holy and without blame as He sees us. God already planned to have us as His own children. This was done by Jesus Christ. In His plan God wanted this done.

We thank God for His loving-favor to us. He gave this loving-favor to us through His much-loved Son. Because of the blood of Christ, we are bought and made free from the punishment of sin. And because of His blood, our sins are forgiven. His loving-favor to us is so rich. He was so willing to give all of this to us. He did this with wisdom and understanding. God told us the secret of what He wanted to do. It is this: In loving thought He planned long ago to send Christ into the world." (NLV)

ACTIVITY: Have a hot chocolate night! Get your mugs prepared before the discussion, as the activity is enjoying your warm drinks as a family while you talk.

NIGHT 2: Have a family discussion over the following Scriptures about receiving the gift of God: Have you received God's gift?

Romans 6:23

"For the wages of sin is death, but the free gift of God is eternal life in Christ Jesus our Lord." (ESV)

Romans 10:9

"...if you confess with your mouth that Jesus is Lord and believe in your heart that God raised Him from the dead, you will be saved." (ESV)

You have the opportunity to pray tonight and receive Christ. You may use this prayer below as a guide, but also feel free to use your own words.

Dear Jesus,
I know that I have done wrong and sinned. I know my sin separated me from You. I can't thank You enough for what You did for me. Thank You for dying and paying for my sins so that I could be with You. I believe You rose again from death, and now I can live with You forever. I trust You as my Savior. Help me live for You as Lord of my life always. In Jesus' Name, Amen

ACTIVITY: It says in Luke 15:10 the angels have a party when someone opens God's gift. With party streamers, balloons, or other fun supplies, have fun as a family imagining God's face when you receive His gift.

NIGHT 3: Read the following Scripture passages and discuss how these truths relate to Christmas, your relationship with Jesus, and the parallels to the storyline of *The Trail of Unexpected Gifts*:

2 Corinthians 8:9

"For you know the grace of our Lord Jesus Christ, that though He was rich, yet for your sake He became poor, so that you by His poverty might become rich." (ESV)

John 14:1-3

"Let not your hearts be troubled. Believe in God; believe also in Me. In My Father's house are many rooms. If it were not so, would I have told you that I go to prepare a place for you? And if I go and prepare a place for you, I will come again and will take you to Myself, that where I am you may be also." (ESV)

ACTIVITY: During dinner, take turns going around the table playing the "That Makes Me Think Of" game. The person who starts the game says a word or phrase, and the next person shares quickly what comes to his/her mind after hearing that word. Each person goes around the table sharing what "That Makes Me Think Of." Go around to each member of the family as many times as you have time to allow for the game.

This fun and interactive game is a good way to practice bringing God's Word and lessons to the forefront of our minds. Try this challenge: Have a sheet of paper as a score card, but instead of individual "scoring" — use this to see how many points you can earn as a whole family. Each of these are surely "wins" for everyone! Be sure to give points for simply funny answers that make the whole family laugh. Put down a tally mark as you play the game if a family member shares something God has taught or shown them. See how many tally marks your family can score, and have fun!

NIGHT 4: Begin with the following verses for family discussion:

Matthew 26:37-39

"And taking with Him Peter and the two sons of Zebedee, He began to be sorrowful and troubled. Then He said to them, 'My soul is very sorrowful, even to death; remain here, and watch with Me.' And going a little farther He fell on His face and prayed, saying, 'My Father, if it be possible, let this cup pass from Me; nevertheless, not as I will, but as You will.' " (ESV)

ACTIVITY: First, discuss what Jesus sacrificed and write notes of thankfulness to Jesus for what He endured for you. Then, together as a family, make a list or draw pictures of ways that you can love sacrificially and extravagantly this year. Choose one or two ways you will intentionally set out to do this in response to God's gift to you. Get out your family calendar and set a date for when you can do this for someone else.

NIGHT 5: Begin your family night reading and discussing these exciting promises:

1 Peter 1:18-21

"...knowing that you were ransomed from the futile ways inherited from your forefathers, not with perishable things such as silver or gold, but with the precious blood of Christ, like that of a lamb without blemish or spot. He was foreknown before the foundation of the world but was made manifest in the last times for the sake of you who through Him are believers in God, Who raised Him from the dead and gave Him glory, so that your faith and hope are in God." (ESV)

Discuss the common phrase, "Happiness can't be bought." While this is true in many situations, I believe you can have happiness and joy knowing that Someone loved you enough to die for you. Therefore, according to 1 Peter 1:18-21...my happiness can be and WAS bought!

ACTIVITY: Have paper and crayons or markers ready for the family. Start your own photo album or Christmas binder of all of the gifts that were meaningful to you throughout the years.

*READ AHEAD FOR TOMORROW NIGHT'S ACTIVITY SO THAT YOU CAN DECIDE
IF YOU WANT TO PREP BEFOREHAND, OR DO IT TOGETHER AS A FAMILY.

NIGHT 6: Discuss and enjoy these two passages of God's love letter to your family:

Colossians 1:15-20

"He is the image of the invisible God, the firstborn of all creation. For by Him all things were created, in heaven and on earth, visible and invisible, whether thrones or dominions or rulers or authorities—all things were created through Him and for Him. And He is before all things, and in Him all things hold together. And He is the head of the body, the church. He is the beginning, the firstborn from the dead, that in everything He might be preeminent. For in Him all the fullness of God was pleased to dwell, and through Him to reconcile to Himself all things, whether on earth or in heaven, making peace by the blood of His cross." (ESV)

Hebrews 12:1-2

"Therefore, since we are surrounded by so great a cloud of witnesses, let us also lay aside every weight, and sin which clings so closely, and let us run with endurance the race that is set before us, looking to Jesus, the founder and perfecter of our faith, who for the joy that was set before Him, endured the cross, despising the shame, and is seated at the right hand of the throne of God." (ESV)

ACTIVITY: Even though it says at the beginning of the book that the gooey sugar cookies were not the announcement that the Christmas season had begun, surely they were a part of the tradition. Personally, if you ask me what treat I think of when I think of Christmas, it is my grandmother's sugar cookies. I've included the famous recipe my family has used for generations, and I would treasure it if your family would adopt it as well!

MRS. MORRIS' SUGAR COOKIES

(Mrs. Applegate's maiden name was Morris, and she received this recipe from her mother)

INGREDIENTS:

1 1/4 C of sugar
2 sticks of softened butter
2 eggs
1/2 teaspoon vanilla

1/4 C milk
1 teaspoon baking soda
3 C flour
1 teaspoon baking powder
1/2 teaspoon salt

Extra sugar for top coating/sprinkling

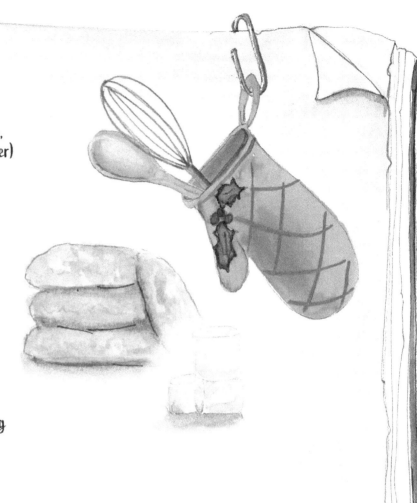

Mix the first four (wet) ingredients.

Gradually add 1/4 C milk to the mixture.

In a separate bowl, sift together the next four (dry) ingredients.

Gradually add the dry mixture to the wet mixture.

Drop by spoonfuls onto cookie sheet. Sprinkle a little sugar on top of each cookie for an extra shimmer and crunch. Bake at 375 for 6-8 minutes (or until slightly golden brown). If you would like to make cutout cookies, leave dough in refrigerator for 30 minutes to 1 hour before rolling out the dough on a surface covered with flour. Bake cut outs for 10-15 minutes.

As you enjoy the cookies, be reminded of the sweetest celebration of God's love!

THE BACK STORY

One day, while traveling back from a family trip, I felt the nudge from the Lord to get an idea down on paper. Grasping for the closest available sheet, I began to scribble out a story board. A white farmhouse and the key themes of what would become this book soon scattered around loose pages from my son's well-loved Lego book (don't worry, I had his permission).

If you saw our home today, you might think that it inspired the story of a family moving to the country. But it was actually a year after I wrote the story, while we were living fine in our city home, that a series of good, "only God" circumstances occurred. He directed us to move, and He led us to a house that looks a lot like the one I drew on those first Lego pages.

When this story first began to take shape in my mind, God put this picture on my heart of a mom and dad trying to figure out how they could afford a gift their child really wanted for Christmas. The scene further unraveled in my mind. After going over the figures, yet acknowledging it would be a sacrifice, the parents squeeze hands and decide "Let's go through with the plan." This phrase echoed in my heart, and the Lord continued adding to the word picture. I began thinking about how the Father, Son, and Holy Spirit were together before creation, and even knowing all that would have to happen and all They would have to give up, They decided, "Let's go through with the plan." We get to sit in this most awesome element of the story of God. He gave so much. He planned and wanted to give everything. You've probably heard the phrase, "Happiness can't be bought." Well, let me tell you this: I think it can. And I think joy can be bought.

<u>1 Peter 1:18-20</u>

"For you know that God paid a ransom to save you from the empty life you inherited from your ancestors. And it was not paid with mere gold or silver, which lose their value. It was the precious blood of Christ, the sinless, spotless Lamb of God. God chose Him as your ransom long before the world began, but now in these last days He has been revealed for your sake." (NLT)

When I think that Someone (and not just any Someone) loved me enough to die for me, that equals happy. That equals joy. Happiness? It was bought for me. It was bought for the person reading this book to you. It was bought for the child listening to this story.

My prayer is that you can read this book with all of your five senses. I pray you hear that God said, "Let's go through with the plan" for you. I want you to taste the pillow-top soft sugar cookies. I want you to feel the warmth of the person next to you on the couch or as you wrestle on your living room rug. I want you to smell what your home smells like at Christmas. I want you to look with your eyes—no matter the living room you are in—and I pray you could daydream. I want you to imagine the Trinity nodding in joyful agreement as They decided long ago that it was a pleasure to give you your present. I want you to experience it all.

And one day we will in full (1 Corinthians 13:12).

ACKNOWLEDGEMENTS

TO MY SAVIOR - Thank You, thank You, thank You, Daddy, for going through with the plan.

TO MY HUSBAND, JOSH - I'm especially grateful to you for excitedly believing in the Lord's hand on this project. Because you dreamed along with me, this book happened. For 20 years, you've taught me how to laugh, persevere and be faithful (full of faith). Thank you, my best friend.

TO HUNTER & PAISLEY - When I told you about the book, you had eyes twinkling like Christmas morning, which will forever spur me on to keep going.

> **HUNTER** - Thank you for the seriously large amount of time you devoted to editing and helping me make this book the best it could be. You cared about it as much as I did, and you really wanted other families to experience the same wonder we experienced as they discovered God's truth.

> **PAISLEY** - Thank you for your enthusiasm and for your dedication to this project. When I had a question or needed your opinion, or an editor, you gave incredibly helpful advice. Thank you for sharing your attention to detail and for the priceless gift of teaching me to imagine. Because of this, you helped other children imagine the "God colors" in this story meant for them (Matthew 5:16 MSG).

TO MY FAMILY AND JOSH'S FAMILY - (whom I am proud to call family, too): Thank you for cheering me on and sincerely being excited with me every step of the way. I am grateful for every Christmas I have spent with you. Thank you for your loyalty. Mom - Thank you for teaching me so much about how to make a home at Christmas for Jesus. Thank you for teaching me the recipe for Mrs. Morris' cookies and for the memories we have every year.

TO CARISSA - Your devotion to this book is like an invitation for every family to attend a much-anticipated Christmas tree lighting. I'm absolutely not exaggerating.

Thank you for wanting to share your talent from the Master Creator by jumping into this project with me. The time you have spent praying, contemplating, and illuminating the story is too many hours to count. Every brushstroke made a difference, and behind every one, I know you believed fully in God's gift of love for each family.

TO ALL OF THE ROBERTSONS - I know you joyfully contributed time and thoughts to help the story—thank you. Thank you for letting your wife (and mom) give to this book. I am truly grateful! Your mom's creativity will leave the readers indelibly happy.

TO THE TEAM AT LUCID BOOKS - Thank you for your encouragement, feedback, execution, and desire for the message in this book. It has been an absolute joy and privilege to work with you. You made it clear from day one that we are all pouring into the same kingdom goal. Thank you for all of your devotion and work to bring this to pass, including your desire to begin this publishing house years ago. Specifically Megan, thank you for walking and creatively brainstorming with me. You saw each detail through from start to finish.

COURTNEY J. STRONG - AUTHOR

Over the years, Courtney J. Strong has told countless adventures of Ralph and Mallory, the original characters in a story series she invented while homeschooling her son and daughter. Now she is thrilled to share these characters with other families.

As a Christian, licensed professional counselor, Courtney guides others to the timeless treasure of childlike faith in God's Word. She is also the author of the women's Bible study, *Preoccupied with Promise.*

The highlight of the week for Courtney and her husband Josh is family ice cream nights on the porch watching a Texas sunset.

CARISSA ROBERTSON - ILLUSTRATOR

Carissa has a passion to use her art to serve the Lord and particularly to connect her art to missions. She has taught art classes in the slums of Nairobi, Kenya and Mumbai, India as well as for refugees settled in the Houston, Texas area. She illustrated a Christmas devotional book in 2018 to which all the proceeds went toward Bible translation.

Carissa lives with her husband and 4 daughters in Houston where she currently teaches art to local school children. She believes that all of us are artists inside and that we were all created to create.

Courtney and Carissa met in a Life Bible Study class in 2004 and have been dear friends ever since.

Printed in the USA
CPSIA information can be obtained
at www.ICGtesting.com
LVHW071144011123
762360LV00060B/713